To: _____

From: _____

Grandma, Grandpa and Me

STUFF KIDS TELL US

COMPILED BY STUART HAMPLE & ERIC MARSHALL

ILLUSTRATED BY ELLEN MUELLER

WORKMAN PUBLISHING, NEW YORK

Library of Congress Cataloging-in-Publication Data

Grandma, grandpa and me: stuff kids tell us/compiled by Stuart Hample
and Eric Marshall; illustrated by Ellen Mueller.
p. cm.
ISBN 0-7611-0767-3
1. Grandparents. 2. Children's writings, American.
I. Hample, Stuart E. II. Marshall, Eric.
HQ759.9.G724   1997
306.874'5—dc21   97-15091
CIP

Cover and book design by Lisa Hollander and Lori S. Malkin
Cover and interior illustrations by Ellen Mueller

Workman books are available at special discount when purchased in bulk for
special premiums and sales promotions as well as for fund-raising or educational use.
Special editions or book excerpts can also be created to specification. For details,
contact the Special Sales Director at the address below.

Workman Publishing Company, Inc.
708 Broadway
New York, NY 10003-9555

Manufactured in the United States of America
First Printing August 1997
10 9 8 7 6 5 4 3 2

CONTENTS

Introduction

What They're Really Like

They Do Some Crazy Things

Worries, Doubts, Questions & Quibbles

Perfect & Not So Perfect

INTRODUCTION

There is something special about the relationship that skips a generation.

For grandparents, there is the opportunity to see again the freshness of life through the eyes of their children's children—those great blessings through whom their dreams live on.

For a child, grandparents are those generous, comfortable folk, who know delicious stories and secrets, who are willing to listen without judgment, and who always seem to have enough time and love to do the things parents are often too busy for. They are, as most children have discovered, a marvelous invention that seems created just for them.

The comments and observations here were collected over a number of years. They reveal certain things children know or feel about their grandparents. They also remind us that grandparents, connecting time past and time present, are a vital part of our history and of who we are. And they are one of God's great gifts.

Stuart Hample and Eric Marshall

What
They're
Really
Like

Grandma and Grandpa have a big garden. He grows the vegetables and she grows the flowers. She eats the vegetables and he smells the flowers. I think that's fair.

Owen, 9 1/2

If you don't have
kids you don't get to
be a grandparent.
That's the deal.

Jeffrey, 8

Being a grandpa is like being president of your family. It's the top job.

Penni, 11

I have a Grandma from France. She speaks English and French. Grandparents can be smart even at their age.

Marie-Helen, 9

My Grandpa is strong and brave. He watches out for you and nobody better try anything if they know whats good for them.

Brandon,
age 8

My grandma gave my mom a very beautiful ring and Someday she is going to give it to me and someday I will give it to my daughter. That's the way you make history.

Brooke, 9

When my mom and dad went away I stayed with my mom's parents. Mom and grandma are the same in some ways — like how they smile and how they make sandwiches.

Muriel, 11

some of them are not
so old, But I think you
are supposed to be
at least 50.

Wendy,
7 1/2

My grandfather comes to all of my ballgames and roots for the team. He always tells me how great I did even when I stink.

Tyler, age 10

You can be a grandma and still have a baby yourself. It's weird but true.

Barbara, 9

Whenever we're at my grandma's house on Friday night she lights the candles and says words in Hebrew. I wish we did it at our house.

Adina, 9

My grandma and grandpa speak mostly Spanish. My mom and dad speak mostly English. I speak mostly both.

Elena, 10

Grandpas and Grandmas are the ones who always love you and never yell no matter how many dumb things you do.

Edward, 10

Some of my friends don't have a grandma. I'm lucky. I even have a great grandma. She works at this big place, a senior center, and complains about the "old people" even though she's 90. And she doesn't even wear glasses!

Sophie, 7

My grandma plays catch with me and she hits good too.

Seth, 9

Grandpa goes out into the garden every morning before anybody else is up and he looks around with that look he has and just dares a weed to come up. He's going to teach me the look.

Raphael, 10

They Do Some Crazy Things

When my grandpa comes over he always says where is Jake and he makes believe he can't see me. He looks all over the house and I sneak around behind him. Then when he gives up I yell Boo and scare him.

Jacob, 7

My daddy says his father would spank him when he was little. Once I asked my grandfather if he use to spank my daddy and he said, "Not enough."

Martha, 10

Sometimes I watch the news with my grandpa. He always gets angry and yells at the TV.

It's lucky they can't hear what he says. Peter.

age 7

My grandma does yoga stuff. She says she doesn't bend as good as she used to but she still does it better than me. Also she can stand on her head

Abby, 9

My grandpa loves to
drink soda. He's the
best belcher in the
world.

Sean, 7

The one thing I don't like about my grandma is they have this photo album with everything in it from when I was a very little baby. One of them is when I don't have anything on and I wish she would take it out of there so nobody could see me naked without any clothes. But she says it is too cute for words.

Aron, 10

Last Christmas when we had a sleepover at grandma and grandpas it snowed so much we had to stay an other day because the electricity went off and we had to use candles and my grandpa made a fire in the old wood stove. It was so cold the water in the toilet froze so you couldnt flush it and that is really cold.

Laura, 11

My Grandma is very nervous. She worries about a lot of things. Sometimes before it even happens. But then it never does.

Richard, 9

My grandparents live in Israel.
He was in the army. So was
my grandma. She's the only
grandma I know who was a
soldier.

Tamara, 9

When we go to a restaurant with my grandpa he always wants to pay the check and my father always tries to grab it away from him but he always loses.

Jessica, 12

When I go to a movie with my granpa he always sleps. Then he says no I wasn't sleeping I was just resting my eyes.

Colin, age 8

On my grandma's birthday she took me out to lunch. We ate outdoors. It was so fun. Then a man said to her how old is your daughter? Grandma said she's my grandaughter. Then he said you're too young to have a grandchild. She said, oh you're just trying to be nice. He said how does it feel to be a grandmother so young? And she said great, better than being a mother.

Renee, 11

My grandpa swims a mile
every day when it's summer.
He goes so slow you would
think he would sink but
he never does.

Karla, 9

I love to watch Grandpa shave. He uses a brush and a lot of shaving cream and sometimes he even puts some on me. My Dad uses a electric razor and that's no fun.

Artie, 8

It's not so great if you go over there on the night they have liver.

Liz, 9

Worries,
Doubts,
Questions
&
Quibbles

You don't have them forever so you have to be careful and also very nice. They know about this too.

Christine, 9

I wonder what grandparents do when your not there. Or when they're not here. I bet not very much because they're always waiting to see you whenever you want.

Laura, 8

My grandmother always asks me how I'm doing in school. And then she says that is very nice but you can do much better. How does she know?

Keisha, 9

My Grandmother gave me a cat. I asked her if the cat had kittens would I be their Grandmother?

Judy, 7

You can't touch anything in grandma's house. you have to wipe your Shoes on the mat every time you come in and you better turn out the lights when you leave the room or else.

Rachel, 10

My Grandpa calls me monkey.
My Grandma calls me honey
even when my freinds are
there. I wish they would
just call me Ben.

Ben — 9

My grandfather is not supposed to eat things with too much salt in them but he loves pickles and he sneaks them when my grandmother doesn't know. If she finds out she gets very very mad and Grandpa gets it good. Then when she's gone he smiles at me and winks.

Alex, 10 years old

Whenever my grandpa comes my mom makes chocolate cake with white frosting because he loves it. But when he doesn't come, all we ever get to eat for dessert is Stupid fruit.

Rebecca, age 10

You have to be very careful with Grandparents. They get sick easy and they can't eat a lot of things but it's worth all the trouble to have them.

Dennis, 9

Grandpas know a lot of good stories and if you ask they will tell them. Sometimes they tell them even if you don't ask.

Michael, 8 year old

The Grandma I have is not really my grandma but I call her that and she is a really good grandma. That's all right, isn't it?

Margaret, 8

I wish my grandma and granpa would live forever.

Lauren, 7 years old

When my grandma was sick they took her to the hospital and I was very scared. They wouldn't let me see her until she went home but I prayed for her it worked. I told her that and then she gave me the biggest kiss in the world.

Wayne, 8

Grandpa listens to the opera when he comes over on Saturday and tells me the story. I like the stories but the other stuff is boring.

Alice 10

When they live far away and send presents you have to write back thank you but that's very hard if you don't like what they send.

Zack, age 10

Perfect
&
Not So
Perfect

Every time I go shopping
with mom she goes fast
and says hurry up, hurry up.
But grandma always has plenty
of time and lets me look
at whatever I want to.

Marietta, 11 years old

Gramma lives in the same house we do only she has her own apartment. We can see her whenever we want to but she always calls us up before she comes to see us. I guess she likes suprises more than mom and Dad do.

Roger, 12

When they come to visit they always tell family stories. We think its neat. But Mom gets mad when they tell funny stuff about her.

Spencer, 10

Grandparents are great because they don't always tell you what you are doing wrong. They just like what you do any way you do it.

Nora, 10

When I'm a grandpa I'll remember all the tricks kids use to get you to do things and I won't let them get away with it.

Max, 10

My grandpa uses a lot of bad words and my granna gets very upset and she says not around the children but it's ok because I know all the words anyway.

Willard, 11

When we go to Grandma's for Easter dinner everyone's there. My Aunts and Uncles and my cousins too. And we eat for hours and hours. You could bust, and everybody shouts and laughs and they tell stories. We have a great time. The food is nice but the laughing and the stories are best.

Kevin, 11

I learned from my grandpa not to wait too long after we eat before I go to the bathroom. Now they can take me anywhere.

Jennie, 7

I had to make a model of a Greek temple and Grandpa showed me how. I cut the pieces and we both put it together. It was fun. He knows all about how to make it. But he lets you do the work.

Brett, 10

I wish they could live
with us. They can have
my room and I can
sleep on the couch
in the living room and
the dog can sleep in
the cellar.

Tori, 7 years old

They never forget your birthday,
They never forget what you want.
If you feel bad they know
how to make you feel
good,
            Emily, 9 years old

I love them because that's what they're there for.

Ashley, 8 years old

You never
know what kind
you will get.
I guess I was
just lucky.

Anne, 9

Inspired by
Helen Hample,
the greatest
grandma
of all,
100 years young
(and counting)